IF YOU WERE A KID DURING THE

American Revolution

BY WIL MARA • ILLUSTRATED BY KELLY KENNEDY

CHILDREN'S PRESS®

An Imprint of Scholastic Inc.

Content Consultant
James Marten, PhD, Professor and Chair, History Department, Marquette University

Photo credits ©: The Granger Collection; 11: World History Archive/Alamy Images; 13: The New York Historical Society/Getty Images; 15: David Lyons/Alamy Images; 17: Don Troiani/Bridgeman Images; 19: MPI/Getty Images; 21: Courtesy Concord Museum; 23: J. James Auctioneers & Appraisers; 25: Don Troiani/Bridgeman Images; 27: H. Armstrong Roberts/Getty Images.

Library of Congress Cataloging-in-Publication Data
Names: Mara, Wil, author. | Kennedy, Kelly (Illustrator), illustrator.
Title: If you were a kid during the American Revolution / by Wil Mara ;
    illustrated by Kelly Kennedy.
Description: New York : Children's Press, an imprint of Scholastic Inc., [2016] |
    Series: If you were a kid | Includes bibliographical references and index.
Identifiers: LCCN 2016009600| ISBN 9780531219713 (library binding : alk.
    paper) | ISBN 9780531221686 (pbk. : alk. paper)
Subjects: LCSH: United States—History—Revolution, 1775-1783—Juvenile literature.
    | Children—United States—History—18th century—Juvenile literature.
Classification: LCC E208 .M3387 2016 | DDC 973.3083—dc23
LC record available at http://lccn.loc.gov/2016009600

All rights reserved. Published in 2017 by Children's Press, an imprint of Scholastic Inc.
Printed in the United States of America 113
SCHOLASTIC, CHILDREN'S PRESS, and associated logos are trademarks and/or registered trademarks of Scholastic Inc.

1 2 3 4 5 6 7 8 9 10 R 26 25 24 23 22 21 20 19 18 17

TABLE OF CONTENTS

4

A Different Way of Life

During the late 18th century, **colonists** in America started a **revolution** against Great Britain. Many people in America wanted the right to choose their own leaders and make their own laws. Imagine you were a kid during the American Revolution. The United States didn't even exist yet. It was just 13 colonies under the control of Great Britain, far away on the other side of the Atlantic Ocean. British soldiers had a strong influence on day-to-day life in colonial towns. Colonists were often treated poorly. But a sense of rebellion was in the air. Many Americans wanted to break free from Great Britain and turn America into an **independent** nation.

Turn the page to visit this amazing time in American history! You will see that life today is a lot different than it was in the past.

Meet Samuel!

This is Samuel Richardson. He is a young boy living in Boston in 1775. Samuel is bright, happy, and curious about many things. His father is a storekeeper who works hard and provides a good living for his family. Samuel likes to be outside when he's not in school or helping out at home. Samuel's cousin Molly is the same age. They go to school together and have been best friends all their lives . . .

Meet Molly!

Molly is Samuel's cousin. She is the daughter of Samuel's Uncle Daniel. She spends a lot of time with Samuel just walking around watching other people live their lives in their busy town. Molly is a bit more courageous than Samuel. She is rarely afraid to speak her mind, and she is always ready for adventure . . .

It was a warm summer evening in 1775. The normally busy town of Boston, Massachusetts, was beginning to settle in for the night. Samuel finished his dinner and went outside to play. Suddenly, he heard the sound of marching feet. He turned and saw a line of British soldiers coming down the road!

MAKING YOUR OWN FUN

Children in the 1700s played with very simple toys. Many were homemade from materials such as clay, wood, or stone. At the time, there were no computers, no video games, and no plastic toys.

This handmade dollhouse belonged to a family in Boston in the 1700s.

Samuel knew the people in his town had been having trouble with British soldiers. He had overheard his father and his Uncle Daniel talking about it. As the soldiers drew closer, he began to get scared. However, the soldiers didn't seem to notice him.

As the soldiers passed by, Samuel heard them talking about his Uncle Daniel. They angrily called Uncle Daniel a **traitor**. This made Samuel even more scared. His father was visiting Uncle Daniel that night!

A COUNTRY TORN IN TWO

In 1775, America was still under the rule of Great Britain. Some people living in America were happy with that. Those people were known as Loyalists because they were loyal to Great Britain. Other people wanted America to have its own government. Those people were known as Patriots.

King George III was the king of Great Britain during the revolution.

Molly was walking around the neighborhood when she saw the soldiers heading toward her home. She knew right away that her father might be in trouble. She had heard him talk about America breaking free from Great Britain. She knew the British didn't like that idea. She began running toward the house.

STOP THESE TAXES!

One of the main reasons people wanted to be free of British rule had to do with **taxes**. Great Britain taxed Americans for many everyday items, including glass, paint, paper, books, and tea. The American people had no **representatives** in the British government to fight these taxes. They became angry about this "taxation without representation."

Stamps like this one were used to mark taxed items in shops.

Meanwhile, Samuel hurried toward his uncle's house. He wanted to warn his father. But he was too late. Samuel moved close to a window to see what was happening inside. The British soldiers were there yelling at his father and uncle. They were treating them both roughly.

Samuel knew he had to do something. As he was trying to think of a plan, someone grabbed his shoulder.

COLONIAL HOMES

A typical home during colonial times was a bit different than the places where most people live today. For example, there was no electricity. This means you would light the house with candles after the sun went down. Also, there was no indoor plumbing. If you had to go to the bathroom, you would use an outhouse.

This house in Massachusetts was built in the 1700s and is still standing today.

Samuel spun around in fear. He expected to see a British soldier. Relief flooded over him when he saw his cousin instead.

"We have to get them out of there," Molly said, still breathless from running.

"But how?" Samuel asked.

Just then, they heard one of the British soldiers tell everyone inside they were being arrested.

"I don't know," Molly said, "but we need to think fast."

NOWHERE TO TURN FOR HELP

In 1775, there wasn't much you would be able to do to stop British soldiers from entering your home. The soldiers were allowed to go into people's houses to enforce British laws. They were not doing anything illegal. On the other hand, by protesting and promoting the idea of independence, the Patriots were breaking laws created by the British government.

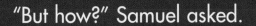

British soldiers were called "redcoats" because of their uniforms.

Molly snapped her fingers and said, "I know what we can do!" Then she explained her plan. They would trick the soldiers and turn the attention away from their fathers.

Molly quickly made her way to the front of the house. Then she yelled as loudly as she could, "Some men are attacking a soldier down the street!"

The British soldiers came out of the house in a hurry. Then they began running in the direction Molly was pointing.

SPEAKING UP

Communication was very simple during revolutionary times. There were no phones or computers. This meant there were also no text messages, tweets, or e-mail. Some places had "town criers" who would shout news as they walked along the streets. People also wrote letters to each other, although the mail system was often unreliable.

In the 1700s, people wrote using pens made from feathers.

Samuel and Molly knew it wouldn't be long before the soldiers realized they'd been tricked. They had to act fast. They went quietly through the back door of the house. When they found their fathers, they led them out into the night.

IN THE DARK OF THE NIGHT

Today, cities have bright lights everywhere to help us see at night. In colonial times, nights were much darker. Some areas were lit with oil lamps. These lamps were lit by hand. Only some parts of the city had them. This would make it easier to stay out of sight at night.

This lantern was used by Patriot Paul Revere during the revolution.

21

Everyone went to Samuel's house. Samuel's dad told his mom what had happened. Once he was done, Uncle Daniel spoke up.

"We should all leave the city," he said. "The soldiers won't stop looking for me, and they know we're related. None of us will be safe."

Samuel's father nodded in agreement. Samuel and Molly couldn't believe they had to leave so quickly. They all agreed to pack up and go.

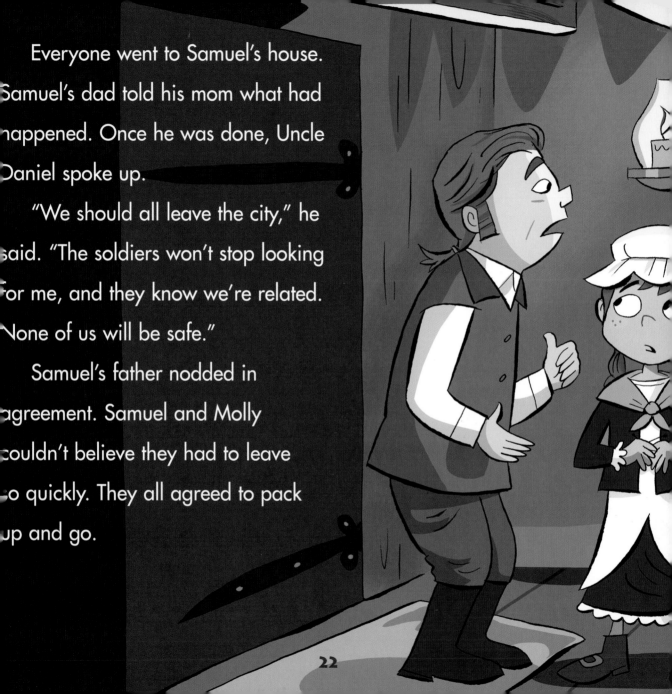

ON THE RUN

In revolutionary times, there were no cars or trains or buses. There weren't even any bicycles. If people wanted to visit friends or go shopping, they either went on foot, on horseback, or in a wagon pulled by horses. For long trips overseas, people had to take ships. The journeys took weeks or even months!

You would sit in a saddle like this one while riding a horse during the revolution.

The family had to walk in the dark for many hours. They left Boston behind and headed for the countryside. Then they arrived at the house of one of Uncle Daniel's friends. He was a fellow Patriot.

Everyone was given food and drink. Samuel and Molly talked about the day's exciting events. While they were chatting, a tall man walked in.

BRAVE FIGHTERS

A **militia** is a group of ordinary citizens who take on the role of an army during an emergency. In the early days of the revolution, American militias frequently fought battles against Great Britain. They were often outnumbered and outgunned. They also did not have as much training as the British soldiers.

Guns used during the revolution had to be reloaded after each shot.

Uncle Daniel shook the man's hand. "This is John," he told everyone. "He's with a local militia."

Uncle Daniel explained how Samuel and Molly had helped them escape the British soldiers at his house earlier that day. John smiled. He told the cousins that he was proud of them.

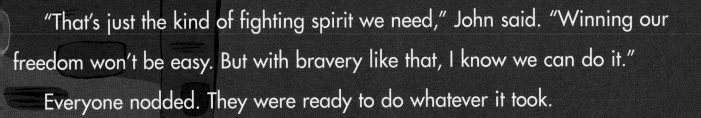

"That's just the kind of fighting spirit we need," John said. "Winning our freedom won't be easy. But with bravery like that, I know we can do it." Everyone nodded. They were ready to do whatever it took.

FIGHTING FOR FREEDOM

The early days of the revolution were hard for the Patriots. There were times when it looked as though Great Britain would win and America would never gain its independence. But the Patriots fought on bravely. Finally, the war ended in 1783. America was free at last!

The first version of the official U.S. flag was created in 1777.

MAINE
(PART OF MASS.)

NEW HAMPSHIRE

NEW YORK

MASSACHUSETTS

LEXINGTON

CONCORD

BOSTON

CONN.

R.I.

PENNSYLVANIA

NEW JERSEY

PHILADELPHIA

MARYLAND

DELAWARE

VIRGINIA

YORKTOWN

NORTH CAROLINA

N

W   E

S

100 MILES

Timeline

1768 British troops begin arriving in America in response to growing unrest among the colonists.

1774 The Continental Congress is formed by American leaders to address unhappiness with British rule.

1775 Battles at Lexington and Concord signal the first military clashes of the revolution.

1776 The Continental Congress issues the Declaration of Independence.

1781 British forces surrender at Yorktown.

1783 The Treaty of Paris is signed, ending the war.

Words to Know

colonists (KAH-luh-nists) a person who lives in a a colony or who helps to establish a colony

independent (in-di-PEN-duhnt) not controlled or affected by other people or things

militia (muh-LISH-uh) a group of people who are trained to fight but are not professional soldiers

representatives (rep-ri-ZEN-tuh-tivz) people who are chosen to speak or act for others

revolution (rev-uh-LOO-shuhn) a violent overthrow of a country's government or ruler by the people who live there

taxes (TAK-siz) money that people and businesses must pay in order to support a government

traitor (TRAY-tur) someone who helps the enemy of his or her country

Index

ABOUT THE AUTHOR

Wil Mara is a best-selling and award-winning author of more than 150 books, many of which are educational titles for children.

ABOUT THE ILLUSTRATOR

Born and raised in Los Angeles, Kelly Kennedy got his start in the animation business doing designs and storyboards at Nickelodeon. Since then he's drawn and illustrated for a variety of children's books and magazines and is currently working on some of his own stories. When not drawing he can be found working on his old cars or playing guitar in a bluegrass band.

Visit this Scholastic Web site for more information about the American Revolution:

www.factsfornow.scholastic.com

Enter the keywords **American Revolution**